LET HER BREATHE

RACHEL REES

FICTION ENGINE

CONTENTS

For Di and Charlie

PART I

TREE TRUNKS

This is what they call me.

So I giggle—they might ask me
to join in and play
if I pretend not to care.

But, they walk past our letterbox
and up the street, laughing
into the distance—

I watch them go without shouting
a word in my defence,
what would I say anyhow?

Instead, I climb up the thick
body of the kōwhai tree
and sit in the fork of the trunk

where two arms splay outward.
I play there with my dolls
until I'm not pretending anymore.

TOWERING DOGS

Have you ever jumped so high off a trampoline you almost touched the stars? Viola did, the day the dogs came. She jumped so high and for so long the soles of her feet grew wet from perspiration. Jumping that high made her feel invisible like Tinker Bell.

In Viola's home her parents often said, "Go to your room, it's adults time now." That meant her dad and mum, and their friends, were going to have a 'joint', or two, or three. With her younger sister in tow, Viola would obediently close her bedroom door, where they imagined ways to surprise. One time they painted each other's faces in leopard spots and tiger stripes. Prepared with convincing meows and roars they pounced into the kitchen. More often than not their attempts would be met with blank stares; this time Viola heard the odd hysterical laugh from behind a swirl of haze.

The family lived in a modest, boxy, 1930s bungalow sectioned off into separate rooms with doors; not like many houses today. In winter the house felt cold like spirit breath. The only exception was the small front lounge with the sticky door handle. It was the largest room, and had a brown-painted brick fireplace that spat and roared all day long, with pinecones and logs that smelled of Tic Toc Road at Rabbit Island. The kitchen was at the opposite end of the house. It wasn't as friendly as the lounge. The walls were a sterile grey, like the hospital, with matching lino floors and lace curtains. There were many cupboards in the kitchen. They started at the lino, covered two walls, and reached ceiling height. Viola barely understood what filled them. Instead, she imagined the jungle gym at school. She pretended she was on a jungle gym island. The lino floor was the Amazon River filled with crocodiles and the cupboard walls were her playground; her monkey bars and trapeze rings. "Don't touch the ground or they'll eat you," she would squeal at her sister, clutching cupboard handles in a frenzy.

Viola liked her room best. Sometimes she camped inside her bedroom under a tent made out of old sheets slung over the backs of dining chairs. She would continue this for days if her mum allowed. Sometimes, when Viola's dad was away with the sea, her mum camped with her. She would nestle in close, and under torchlight Viola would read her mum bedtime stories until they fell asleep.

The day the dogs came, Viola didn't hear her mum answer the front door. The first sound that filtered through her ears was a chorus of strained yelps from her bedroom tent—so close she could smell their excitement. And the voices: "We have a warrant to search your house." What felt like a tremble at first erupted into a stampede that shook the floors. Dogs. Towering dogs. Their eyes were empty yet focused, their nostrils flared and runny. They pulled at their collars. They knew what they wanted. Sniff, sniff and find the truth. Find the drugs. Find the proof. From one room to the next—sniff, sniff, sniff! They were attached to mean-looking adults. The adults' eyes were wild and they chewed gum with clenched teeth. Viola's mum cursed as three uniformed adults pushed her down the hall, out of Viola's sight. Where is Mum? Viola worried. Her heart was beating to the rhythm of the roaring fire and she couldn't breathe through the tears. She heard her mum sob. She was pleading, "Please don't, I don't have anything." The jarred force of drawers and cupboards being torn apart sent hot shivers up Viola's spine. Then, the dogs entered her bedroom. She ran out of her tent and past their hot determination, to be with her mum.

Mum is beautiful like a jasmine vine. She wears soft Indian skirts with gathered waists and white muslin shirts; her feet bare. Her hair is spicy like gingerbread. It falls in cascades around her face, and her eyes are deep and sparkling like a calm ocean. She hugs Dad for the longest time before he leaves for the sea and when he returns she is so happy she cries. In summer we ride our bikes to the river. I hold onto Mum as she dives under the water and together we drift between the water weed like mermaids. Sometimes Mum's face changes shape. She appears from the kitchen, smoke billowing behind her, and I don't know if she is happy, angry or sad. She warns me to leave her alone, go to my room, and play. I don't understand and so I cry. She gets angry. Her face changes shape again and again and I'm so confused I run into my room and slam the door behind me. I hide in the wardrobe and wait until the jasmine flower blossoms again.

Viola entered her parent's bedroom. Her mum was sitting hunched over the end of the bed, her body stripped down to underwear, arms wrapped around her breasts. Three police officers stood around her; one was writing onto a large clipboard with a sharp pencil. Her face was grey like the kitchen; her eyes wild like the fire. Viola ran back into her bedroom, opened the wardrobe door, crept inside, and wept.

It was hours before Viola saw the kitchen lino again. A whole Four Square store had been dumped into the Amazon. Even crocodiles wouldn't have been able to survive. The cosy lounge with the spitting fire now resembled a barren wasteland with barely a trace of spark. Viola sat on the front door step with their well-meaning next-door neighbour, eyes and ears fixed on the dawn chorus. "You need to be strong for your mother," she said as she stroked Viola's back with her warm hand.

Some of Viola's neighbourhood friends stared at her as they walked past on their way to school. They spoke to each other in low hushed voices but

Viola knew what they were saying. "I'm not going to school today," she said to her next-door neighbour. "I'm going to play on the trampoline."

The trampoline sat waiting on the newly mowed section of lawn in front of the house. The lawn was bordered by a wide concrete edge with colourful flowers in organised rows that her mum had planted a few days before. Viola squinted and shook her head. Nothing seemed to make sense. She climbed onto the steel coil rim and scrambled onto the slinky surface of the mat. She jumped higher and higher, the front garden blending with the sky; a kaleido-scope of flowers and blue. She jumped until new pictures emerged—her world changing shape again and again. Soon she was flying like a fairy among the stars. Her eyes empty yet focused like the towering dogs.

THE SMELL OF RETURN

His arms outstretched
His smile
His navy sailcloth bag
pinned against his back
like a shell—

And it rained before

The tarmac smells hot
A remarkable, white heat
shipwrecked on the road—

I stand at the brown gate
beneath the kōwhai tree
one arm shading my face from the sun
as yellow flowers, like bells,
sway before my eyes—

He arrives at the gate
Rests his right hand on my head
I lock my child arms around his waist
and breathe in—

His sweat, like hot tarmac
His rum and cigarette breath
His fish, sea and salt-weathered sweater.

OBSERVING THE WORLD

From way up here
on the roof of the garage
as high as a mountain
I am the girl observing the world

The world from up here is easy, like eating
It is the place I come to read, and pretend and dream

On the ground, the world is hard, like talking
It is the boy you like, and a mean best friend

On the ground, grown-ups
do things I swallow up—

My mother
she sunbathes, a cigarette dangles from her lips
coconut butter and nicotine smells waft through the air

Our neighbour, Mrs Gravy
She watches *Days Of Our Lives*
slouched back, with stomach rolls, in her lazy-boy chair

And Mrs Biddy, the pensioner
outside her flat, bent over—
she steals my cat with chunks of horse liver

This observing of the world goes on
without deeper study of the meaning
the 'why?' and 'what for?'
only the grown-ups reason is right

That's what being a child is like—
it's all input and memory stored
without the logic that states:
Everything is, or is not, ok.

IMPACT

When Rory was fifteen
A pumped up scholarship boy
Said he didn't like her
Said it sarcastic as high tone microphone feedback
Said she was nothing but trash
as he pushed her to the riverbed by her neck
Said he would teach her class rules
as he forced his prize on her like blood-clot.

Now each time she begins a conversation with a man
she endures the hidden ringing of interference in her ears.

HELLO VOICE

Hello voice
are you there?
If so, where?

EPIPHANY IN THE STEAMED UP GLASS OF THE SHOWER

She takes the tripod, twists it onto the camera, sets it up beside her bed and presses the timer button. She then stretches out on the bed—pale fleshed and goose pimpled—and looks into the lens until the light flashes.

She prints out the picture on a sheet of glossy A4 paper and looks at herself naked.

She begins slicing into the photo, using a pair of stainless-steel sewing scissors—each arm becomes elbow, forearm and wrist; each breast delicately removed. Lips, nose, each eye and each ear also dissected.

Finally, she draws the scissors toward her skull, and seeing a cauliflower pattern where hair should be, carefully severs each river and valley.

She stands back to observe the crudeness of her handy work and thinks, "This is who I was."

It was while showering, she remembered. She had an epiphany as she looked at the 'whole' of herself in the steamed up glass of the shower. So vivid was this moment, this one revelation that she is indeed a whole person.

It was as if an eyelash had scratched the surface of her eye.

HURT

I can turn it on
and off like any
kitchen appliance.

NEW LAND

Life held her captive under the ship deck
Held her down there with the rats and the echoes

She had heard of far-off places:
of white, red, and black sands
She had stolen glances from commanders

Ripped out sheets of lost treasure
Had cursed the night time and the anchor

Each night she prayed for new land
New land under the surface of the ocean

where guitars are only ever acoustic
and stars line the sea floor. Where

bubbles are refuge for waterlogged souls
and sea turtles carry solemn seafarers on their shields

On the last night of winter
as the echoes and the rats slept

She scaled the ladder to the bow of the ship
Climbed up the mast

Against the force of the wind
Higher and higher to the topmost point...

and she jumped.

APOLOGY TO THE ONE

If you ever meet
The One
in the corner, seeing double
while you're propped in destitution
on the far end of Mollies or Taylor's or
(God forbid) the
Grumpy-Mole bar

And if you ever catch a movie with
The One
and he drives you home in his parent's car
then waits too long,
so you're challenged to kiss him
but you weren't quite ready

And if you ever draw a pros and cons list
about The One
yet decide the larger list of cons
is worth ignoring,
because you've never been loved
like this before and need it

And if you ever sign your name
next to The One
on a mortgage agreement
that should have read travel itinerary
which seems sensible at 19—
(bless them) your parents are so proud
and it IS the right thing to do

And if you ever feel love
for The One
like the tender embrace from a dear friend
with benefits that show an honest face
but on any other day
leave you frigid

And if you ever submerge those thoughts

of The One
as a lead weight tied to a balloon would
only to rise to the surface
and be forced under again

And if you ever say yes
to The One
and it was *you* who called it
stumbling home on the first new morning
Watties tom and sesame seeds
grouted to the edges of your big mouth

And if you ever say I do
in reply to The One
while holding his hand
and reciting Kahlil Gibran
(the bit about the two oak trees)
and you actually think you've created
the perfect day

And if you ever quit your job
against The One's noble wishes
praying 'this will be the solution'
to your silent weeping
because you're really still a girl
who should've travelled

And if you ever find yourself
leaving The One
the only agreement chosen
marked
Separation of assets
as if it were a black eye on his heart
absinthe left to writhe in his mind
while you sip peppermint tea.

And if ...

Well, then you know.

PART II

DOWN THE ROAD

Removed from my old life.
It's been a year.
Footsteps and wheels
left behind. Cockroaches,
a relentless mosquito;
dogs bark—
I hear them down the road.

SHE CARRIES A WOODEN HEART

She sees her birth father on a jetty near Tryphena—
He wears dark glasses, she
has a wooden heart tied around her neck.

They drive inland toward Awana Bay
over the sloped ridges of Aotea Road,
taking turns as they approach his home—
She of the dreams: the seaside house
with a black-lacquered baby grand
and the sweep and curl of an unknown bay, like a lick.
He of their likeness: how her brow line
pinches in sunlight

and the way she smiled just before when
he said he was unaccustomed to visitors
and a loner of sorts.

Three nervous days wheel by.

Brahms moves along the strings of his old cello
each morning of each day. He plays
the way the rain sounds in the trees—
impatient but poised, droplets of pure beauty.

She imagines she's a genius daughter living the poet's life
in a ramshackle house
with Bunsen burner cookers
and crayons scattered over the dining table.

She is dreaming reality.

At times, she thinks of giving her heart to him
but twenty-seven years holds her back.

He has five children to four separate women
and is still counting.

HOPE GLITTERS ON GREEN GRASS

I stand at the junction of thirty-first and second street; my empty hands cupped together willing the pigeons to drink. My eyes are dilated, mascara smudged into streams; my ripped stockings and an oversized coat unsettling pedestrians. They sidestep the oily puddle that might stain their shoes and continue up the avenue without glancing back. I smile as I cry. Over the road in Johnsonville Park I see a glittering on the field of green like sunbeams over Hudson River. I want to go to its calling, but high fives and wolf whistles remind me of last night when life turned black under stars that shone so bright. I love the light. It calls to me, crawls through me, shields me from the fright, when blinged-up boys on the basketball court stained my dress, my heart, my faith in life. I walk to the edge of the park. And I walk to the edge of my heart. Where a ring was lost among green blades so black last night. The chance of finding the ring seeps in under my skin. I bend down and pretend to slide the ring on my wedding finger. I lie on my back and let the feeling linger. I feel my coat drop away from my shoulders and the stockings vanish from my legs. Closing my eyes, I rest.

TWENTY-FIRST CENTURY LOVE

I meet you
Stare at your face
I feel you or I don't, and it's real, baby
I can tell this just by looking, no words spoken
I listen on a different level
With organs, skin, heart palpitations;
with the hair on the back of my neck
sweat beads on the palm of my hand
I feel it, baby
and it makes me want to howl.
But look into me
Look through and into the
rabbit hole, the
black hole, the
white light—
Like a clear water puddle, I am your reflection
Now do you want to cum over me?
Open your mouth
just wide enough for one finger—
Feel it slide in and
touch your tongue—
There I am, and it is real, baby
I'm at the tip of your tongue like that misused word,
love.

LOVE IS A SIGN ON A PLANE

YOU SHOULD KNOW BY NOW
flashed above her head.

Bold, red letters on the tongue of her mind.
Stung with pride she nursed her ego
with a G&T while the flight attendant
read the emergency instructions.

She felt the cool steel pinch
as the belt clicked into place.
LEFT, RIGHT, EXIT, the neon arrows flared.

She was over him and his obsession
with The Cure.

I ariv at 5,
the text message read.

In her mind she kicked the seat
in front of her.

EXIT—the neon flashed.
EXIT!

All she read was LOVE.

BRAVE

When you said I was brave to live with him,
to live with him "as friends"
you said it with inverted commas
I felt the muscles in my back tense a little—
I understood your sincerity, yet couldn't help but think,
what is brave about living with someone you love?
Then I remembered what had been—
April through October
Three times he had told me
I was not, "Her"
Three times he had said
he didn't feel, "that way" about me
It happened mostly under the sheets too,
our bodies locked tight.

You are right.
I am brave, in spite of words.

I liken this experience
to the cross-country races we ran
at Intermediate School
I was eleven perhaps,
overweight and shy

Teachers didn't speak of well-being back then.

As I choked along the dusty reserve,
able kids streaked ahead
My mind would fast-forward and rewind
the same defeating statements:
'You can't handle it,' and,
'You're not good enough.'

I would slow down until barely walking,
my head working against my spirit.

But I would finish.

Second to last perhaps, but I would cross
the finish line.

THE NATURE OF THINGS

Moth of the moon—

You entered my bedroom
Then my mind
It was a warm, mid-February night

You rested your fragile body
on the page of the dictionary
I had open at nature *n.*

Your paper-thin legs clutched the spine
Powdery wings stretched
toward the desk lamp light

I typed your nature in and out
desperate to pin you down

You became the figure
of Amores: two loves for my heart
The winged Boreas
Livas at the sternum
then an angel I did not yet deserve

But before I unravelled myself
and captured your myth,
short as a passing glance, you left—

And so did the words.

The substance of this poem
the open page of the dictionary

The gap between each meaning
spelling out the nature of things.

HALOS OF THE NIGHT

She ruminates
over Walton's 'Categories of Art' theory:
the concept of properties in aesthetics of art.
Of standard and variable and contra-standard qualities
that might give her the sensation
of falling in love
if she let said properties in.

This is how she wants to feel right now
of course, instead of dumped.

She scans the white walls
of the big space
called the gallery.
A series of photos taken
by someone important
hang in the gallery.
Images of windows, chapels and steeples,
gun-shell-fire and glass, and children—
she sees them
yet she's not crying
or even close. Instead
she's cursing the artist, the gallery
and yes,
even God for her lack of feeling.

It's not human is it, this unfeeling?
Is this what they call writers block?

A blocked drain
A blocked one-way-street
A blocked nose

A girl stands at a lean
by the Rua Nova whatever.
Her cropped, banged,
swept-to-the-side
white blonde

tinted bob
has variable properties
which are aesthetically pleasing.
But this example before her
does not feel inside of her
like it might.

She is about to leave when she is stopped
by eight sooty Moreporks:

They wear coalface feathers
and carry intent in their eyes.
Squat together on perches
behind a window of glass,
they look out at the white walls and the big open space
lined by the strangers who scrutinise.

She decides their properties are standard.
They are stuffed.
Yet, when one winks at her,
she feels a pinch of emotion
as if it had noticed she was in disguise:

To all the onlookers—

those searching and reflective faces in the room
who puzzle and question
and ah …
and ooh …
We see life in your shadows
and dark places in your light
We chant the melancholy hooting you hear
We are halos of the night.

– inspired by the photography of Laurence Aberhart.

OUT CAME THE SHINE

It began like a repetition
Like an incy wincy premonition
She weaved a room of lace curtains
And he climbed up the water spout
And he dried up all the rain—

Though for realism's sake
Let's not pretend this is a story about spiders
knights or rings and posies
It was a person who spun into the room
And laughed and loved too soon
He pulled a tendril in her web
And she tumbled down—

She had emptied all her pockets
Dried up all the shame
Put on her armour
And had begun to climb again
When he announced his departure
Left the washing unfolded on the chair—

You would think it stirred up insecurity
Of living as a widow
But this lady wasn't dead
Instead, she climbed in her imagination
It washed out all the pain
Yes, he left before the sun had dried up all the rain
But out came the shine and the posies did bloom—

Now the premonition
The incy wincy repetition
Can begin yet again.

SALACIOUS ACTS

It was all about him
And I felt quite calm
Seemed like harmless fun, really

Then night fell dark
And a dozen blankets
Couldn't stop the shivering I felt

What was he seeing?
In veiled light
Beneath a swampy stirring of pinot and hops

Bless him and his pipe dreams
The salacious escapist
With young in the womb

I pity those rough kisses
Placed upon love's lips

No place for tenderness
Just a rough hand
On her breast

SELF-PORTRAIT ON WINDOW SEAT

She's huia
with broken wing
and stolen tail feather

Landed
on the open window sill
below the seat of her home,
the deforested hole
left to her after conquest

She is bent and wild
recoiling in fear of what comes next

Unable to swoop or squawk or fly

but she'll try.

PART III

ALARM

She knew things would be fine, but

the air felt sad and her mood wilted
like the cherry blossom
at the end of its cycle—

Release the pain, hold it inside, laugh
there's really no telling—

death and love is so close to her

She woke—as usual—
to the sound of her alarm.

RECLAIMING YOUTH

Or is it remembering boredom?

This isn't as easy as first thought

Boredom, I would hope, shouldn't suggest
I did nothing with my youth,

sure, stuff did happen—

Perhaps I should go to a hypnotist,
draw out the details?

All I remember
is the past ten years trying to get better

Before that
seems like
a series of vignettes—60 second film reels
with moth holes chewed into them.

BEFORE DIFFERENCE

I want to remember you
and me as children. Before
we were bodies in the moonlight.

I imagine the playground at school:

There's me—I'm at one end
making daisy chains for friends
and you're on the swing
over there
with your legs kicked high

And hey!
There's you at show and tell:

You're in a pressed and buttoned shirt
playing something beautiful
on a beaten-up piano

a couple of keys are out of tune

and there's me again

I'm at the back
singing all the words
under my breath.

SURVIVAL RESPONSE

1

The road divvied up farmland and suburb.
Its length was a hop, skip and
crack-is-a-rat
from Saxton to Quarantine.
A thin, barbed-wire fence on one side
was secured on rough-sawn,
lichen-crusted timber posts,
whacked in, uneven along the boundary.
The road developed at great speed.
First to go were the lambs and horses, and then
the barns and the hay and the green.
In their place plumb fences
and prefab pavements and topiary trees
protected by green wrought iron
and tricolour pansies.

A young girl wrote a story about baa-lambs on neigh-land
and sleeping under stars on the steel coil trampoline.

2

At the spoon end
of a quiet
hilltop cul-de-sac,
a woman noticed a lamb grazing
on the neighbour's lawn.
She walked down the concrete path
in her dressing gown, slippers on.
They scuffed an echo
as the sun rose over an orange and pink sea.
The lamb had strayed from
the subdivided lifestyle block of pale grass,
to the residential side of the harakeke and gorse.
She wanted to hold the lamb; wanted to feel its body,
stroke its ears, and smell the tufts of wool.

She heard its hooves scratch the pavement
as it scrambled away, all out of rhythm.
She heard it call.

THAT GIRL

I was always that girl. The one at the front swaying beneath the band. I'd be dancing for attention, swishing my hips from side to side as I gazed at the bassist, as if he was smouldering at me, as if he was interested. The night would blur into thin bands of bright neon. The beer fridge would buzz under pressure from the crowd who were much louder and tackier than the floor. By the time we'd hit The Outback, *Ace of Base* pumped out in some Brit-pop remix, I'd be bumping my ass into the guy behind me and it felt so hot and real and even romantic. I never left with any of those guys though; the three am mince pie and chips held more appeal back then. I'd waver back and forth at the Circle K blowing steam into my hands, my eyelids dropping like a stone in water, while bits of pastry rubbed between the corners of my chapped lips. Yep, I was that girl. The one who cried into the toilet and dribbled saliva and snot at the same time; who fell asleep in her clothes and woke with contact lenses still in. The morning after girl, the complete write-off girl with a headache and cravings and foul language and all that. Lying outside all day on a coil sprung mattress in my pyjamas eating junk like *Twisties* and laughing uncontrollably until I snorted—you know how.

And here I am now watching that girl all over again. She's brave, I hear someone say. By jove, that girl, she's carefree. She's dancing for everyone, swishing her hips and clapping her hands and yelling "Woohoo". She's a real hoot. She's happy isn't she, they say. The bassist is watching her like he's on drugs. And I'm watching all this and I crack up. She's so sweet, waving about like that. Like she's the only person there and the music is playing for her and the lights are bouncing off the walls for her. She's that girl. The one who'll cry into the arms of the bouncer this time and her mother sometimes and her cup of tea other times and into her knees at night while in bed. She's also the girl that someone will give a baton to and yell Run!

And she will. For as long as she can, or until she sees her partner, and then she'll pass the baton on, but until then she'll run up and down hills of lessons. She'll run to the edge of the world she has created, look back and then she'll jump. Lucky for her the ocean will break her fall and she'll bob up and down taking in the cool silence. A dolphin will push her up. The surge of water will awaken her and for once she'll think "I'm alive" and then she'll want to die because she's that girl. She's so vulnerable and powerful it kills other people and they hate her for it but love her at the same time. And she knows how they feel but what can she do right? She's that girl. Growing weary of her treading, the sea creatures will tell her to find her own place. They'll leave her on the pebbles to dry off. In the sun she'll lie, watching the nerves in her eyelids wiggle about like a germinating seed about to burst through the dirt. Beads of water on her skin will evaporate and she'll pick herself up and ride a lonely bike back to town. Waiting for her arrival will be a letter saying "Congratulations, you won" and she'll faint. Yep, she's that girl.

CHAMELEON SKY - *A HAIBUN*

I

I cycle along the backroads of Oamaru. The wind is warm and dry. I see the nakedness of the Southern Alps. Summer's drought has crept into autumn to hurt this land. Parched fields lay dormant. Dust topples over the dirt road like a string of falling dominos. I turn into Homestead Road and swoosh down the roly-poly hillock into greener land where the maple trees sing. I return home to find mum sitting in her chair watching the ocean. Rex, their neighbour, has passed away.

> Fields of dry and gold
> Tense gorse bushes hitch
> —Stop please!
> We will go anywhere.

II

Today, couples hold hands and walk along Thames Street admiring hokey-pokey buildings with their old-world charm and tall, chiselled columns. Highland bagpipers stand outside the Criterion pub. I cycle into Harbour Street market and wave to the organ manufacturer. Maple leaves along Tyne Street scatter like a restless sleep. The smell of the old train tracks evokes a feeling of being in another time when coal was mined for survival and people stowed on trains and fishermen had curly moes and carved pipes and newspaper boys wore cheesecutter hats. At the edge of the cliff I stop and watch Oamaru from the shoreline.

> Penguin colony—
> Herring gulls rest.
> Still gentle
> the quiet shoreline.

III

While sleeping, heavy rainfall filled the flats of the town. I see swimming pools where parks and fields once lay. Houses evacuated, schools closed and the postal service abandoned until it is safe again. We are Noah's Ark on the hill. Mum puts the phone receiver down. Mourners from Dunedin have cancelled plans to attend Rex's funeral. Says he didn't like a fuss.

Roberts Park is clear
Orana is under siege
Swallowed
in new rain.

IV

Was it inevitable that I would come here? Will my parents' cigarette smoke affect me later in life? Will I really end up with a hunchback if I don't invest in a proper chair? Can I keep up with his high sex drive? What should I have for breakfast? What's *really* more open – a small town or a city? Where has Rex gone? Will I ever look at myself and be content?

Chameleon sky
I watch it turn
Swift and still
Writer's knotted mind.

A REFLECTION POEM

We sit on the couch with tea and ginger nut biscuits
and between slurps and laughing, we agree
our friendship has come to the point of relating
where words are superfluous
We're wiser
We're at the point where we can look and see the other—
The past and its jealousy, envy, admiration, and growth
between us, in us, and out in the blue and green,
on islands, on continents
The present as it is now, wordless, yet rich with script
crafted as fables
And the future, how mysterious it is, and will be

How is it we were this fortunate to meet one another?
How is it we are fortunate enough to remain friends?

These are questions with many hundreds of answers—
a city, a state, a country's worth—
it seems it just *IS* that we sit here now
and through it all, you know,
the folding and unfolding of time,
we have stayed symbiotic as flowers and insects.

CHEMISTRY

How I love chemistry and physics and all of science!

Since child time, I've felt I were part of something greater,
something perhaps spiritual but too obscure to talk of here

Something only chemistry and physics
and the heavens know.

PART IV

TIPS OF TOES

I once believed
we walked the earth
on equal footing
on equal terms

Now I see
we struggle across sand
on our heels
or the tips of our toes.

FALLING BRIDGES

I'm on a cobbled bridge
It falls away
at each new step I take—

Never again will I walk
over its arch
and peer into the river below—

And where am I going?
To a waterfall
and mountains
there's no-one at my side
but a small boy in red,
his chocolate coloured belly
round and sticking out, he knows
he is love, like me—

I walk on a treadmill
of crumbling pebble,
picking daisies to lace into my hair—
To my right
there's a lion and an elephant
but there are no flies—

Instead,
and the boy knows too,
our lives are falling bridges
and the fear of not remembering
is a dark tunnel that I never enter:

"Made of earth?" the boy asks.
"Yes," I reply, "A dry, brittle jigsaw of dirt."

THE GREAT NEW ZEALAND LAPDOG

I could crawl on my hands and knees
a leash and collar strapped to my neck,
and be pulled into line
for direction—

Stop, wait, wait,
lie down, roll over,
fetch, go on, fetch,
play dead.

I could stand naked
in the vanity mirror,
shaving day-old stubble
I could dress as if 'I am'
in Armani (at best, the jacket)
I could drive an SUV along tree-lined streets,
just wide enough
I could work for Saatchi and Saatchi,
making headlines and enhancing lives
At lunch, I could talk
of my property acquisitions
and the bottom line in profit
(we are talking about home ownership, remember)
and I could 'hear, hear' corporate ownership
as the way forward for New Zealand.

Yes, I could—

And I'd bark
I'd bark like a dog for that.

ASH LANDS RHYTHM

It is easy | to focus | on what is wrong
There is much in this world that is twisted
Limbs bent like paper clips, splintered
body parts swimming in streets
and in fields, decaying on hospital beds

Families separated in the opal night sky—

It is easy | to focus | on the path of right
to cheer the mouths of the red, white and blue,
who spew—

You can't stop me
I'm hope from the sea
I forgive your shame
Now play the game

It is easy | to listen | to ash lands rhythm
Yes, opposites do exist, there is dark and light

It is easy | to shut down | to the sound of love
fear strikes deep
it maims and stains
it is a red hot language
that kills language
it kills

And language?
It is a blessing!

The language of birds | their high-pitched verbs
the swoop and soar of flight
The language of people | uniting cultures
bridging gaps in understanding

It is a blessing | It is a blessing | It is a blessing, right?

The language I see on the news today

blows ash across the names
faces and worlds of our children
yet they respond in wonder, they taste it,
not yet aware of the bitter.

To hell with this war!
This spending of life will not do
Our children are being carried away
into revolution, revolting,
rebounding and trigger hounding—

I do not know him.
I do not know man anymore.

THE CICADA

And there, on the pavement, was the cicada.
No clamorous song, the cicada was silent.

I remember mountains of cicadas that morning:
many were shells, splintered and waxed as gardeners' fingernails;
some were crushed into a gunk,
their severed wings flapped in Wellington's habitual breeze.

I remember the strangeness of summer that year:
the southerlies and the bullet rain,
more southerlies, and a fumy heat.

I remember thinking: those cicadas are like soldiers.
They had flown into battle
sending out coded messages from their tymbals.
Then, stealthy on the sides of telegraph poles,
they fell from intoxicating weather to the pavement below,
each severed wing a broken limb.

That evening, in wonderment,
I watched as my cat brought in a cicada.
It was alive with clicking!
It was singing—

I remember instant fear for the cicada's powerful muscle
as she bit into its abdomen with her teeth.
Its final muffled message
like Dream of a Witches Sabbath:
the theme song from a psychological thriller
played out before me.

Perhaps some kind of peace was restored
and her action simple—downright biological.
It was only a cicada, after all…
But for me, it was not simple.

I remember a wet and windless autumn

and with it a flawless pavement.
I still can't stomach the thought of it.

THE WIND

A cat
wraps around
herself like a bun,

ears pricked
to the gargle
on the radio

and your manic
enthusiasm—
her simple life

mocked
by irascible wind.
It is coming

to dusk, the light
tells me so—
darkened clouds

hurdle
the handsome face
of the Makara range,

burdened with
a message for the city
and the sane.

Rooftops stiffen.
Leaves like hands
scatter.

I stand
at the bare window
confuse the wind

in my Frida-Kahlo-red

circle skirt
pen to skin.

57

SOMETIMES I NEED TO RISK LOSING MY PLACE

Without a place—that physical space
we trace into shapes from ampoules
filled with hard-fought blood.
And without geographical boundaries—
those legitimate fence-posts
and border controls bordering us
from the blue of our own sea.
And without the mental capacity
for emotionality—the feeling
that tells us when we've crossed a line
in our circling lives,
stamped out with sedatives
from over the counter policy.
Without these false securities,
what would the rules of place be?
And, who drew the line on the ruler?
What sense of entitlement determines our periphery?
How dare they yell: "Stop, no entry!"

Sometimes I need to risk the uncertainty—
Sometimes, I need to allow that person
to jump ahead of me—
Sometimes, I need to sacrifice
my position by the tallest widest expanse of window—
Sometimes I need to let go in the argument,
forgo argument's ugly scrutiny—
Sometimes, I need to distance myself from the
pain in the world so it doesn't consume me—
Sometimes, I need to lose my place
on the page of memory.

PART V

LET HER BREATHE

How do you tell her?
You may feel scared
because you are a woman now.
But always the girl with permission to dream.
And dreams are free—
they are free.
How do you tell her?

How do you warn her?
Life is metamorphosis.
Sometimes perilous.
We walk unmarked roads
every day, and only
some of us will find our heroes.
Others will have theirs delivered.
How do you warn her?

How do you deliver her to spirit?
The prescription of her
being on this earth;
when worldviews fly like daggers
and they scar her alive.
How do you deliver her to spirit?

How do you give back her dignity?
There is little dignity
in a world of parchment and men.
It is discrimination for some
and cruelty for others.
How do you give back her dignity?

How do you do all this?
Can I say you don't?
And it is for love you don't.

You don't tell, warn, deliver or give back.
It's not for anyone to do these things.

Just believe in her chosen womanhood,
and dream with her chosen womanhood,
and inspire her into her chosen womanhood—

and in doing this
let her breathe.

TALLULAH

You are precious
unique and new

You are love
so pure so true

Life awaits you
so live it in full

Grow your voice
Miss Beautiful.

EPILOGUE

THANK you for taking the time to read to the end of this book. If you feel like writing a review or adding a rating, that would mean the world to me. Simply choose your favourite platform from Goodreads, Amazon, Kobo, Apple Books or Google Play. You can keep in touch with me via email: rachel@rjrees.com

Love,
Rachel x

ACKNOWLEDGMENTS

Heartfelt gratitude to Penelope Todd for reading many of these poems, without compensation, in the winter of 2013. Her kindness, encouragement and suggestions have been priceless. Enormous thanks to Cliff Fell who steered me into writing poetry in the first place, offered his unwavering support and guidance during my break-out Creative Writing year back in 2006, and who wrote in support of my successful application to IIML in 2014 of which I didn't pursue in the end. Gratitude also to Jessica Le Bas who rallied me to 'dig deeper', Rachel Bush who provided feedback of my CREW 253 folio submission, and Chris Price who wisely reminded that "You don't stop being a writer when you hand in your folio!" - I stopped, but I'm back. A virtual hug for each and every writer who has inspired me, from my writer comrades at NMIT to fellow poets at Victoria University and the many accomplished souls who "sit inside the burning bush". Finally, extra love and thanks to Edwin McRae, my honey, my best friend, my editor and biggest fan (and I his).

NOTES

The structure for *Let Her Breathe* was inspired by the poem *Autobiography in five short chapters* by Portia Nelson, from the collection *There's a Hole in my Sidewalk: The Romance of Self-Discovery.*

Earlier versions of Tree Trunks, Before Difference, Survival Response, The Cicadas, and Towering Dogs have been previously published.